DEDICATION

To our loves and love of this magical place, an anchor

for our lives; ever changing; one continuous burst of light,

color, wind, fog, water, joy and companionship.

ACKNOWLEDGEMENTS

Our heartfelt thanks go to Todd M. LeMieux for graphic design;
Paul Lindale, Michelle Johnson and Wayne Medeiros for com-
puter assistance, Judith Neeld for editing and Elizabeth Norcross
for art commentary. Some versions of poems have appeared in
Stone Country and *The Vineyard Gazette*.

First Edition
Second Printing 2000
ISBN 0-9645250-2-X

A

MAGICAL

PLACE

poems, paintings and photographs
of
Martha's Vineyard

POEMS BY BROOKS ROBARDS · ARTWORK BY NANCY PURNELL

TABLE OF CONTENTS

~

Foreword: In the Decades of the Seasons 6

The Ceremony of Arriving 8

Opening the Summer House 10

Summer's False Start 12

On-Island 14

A New Season 16

Nor'easter 18

Early Morning in Oak Bluffs 20

Plaisir d'Amour ne Dure qu'un Moment .22

Longest Day of the Year 24

Wind Watch in Oak Bluffs 26

Vineyard Fog 28

Stanley Burnshaw Puts His House on the Market 30

Solitude 32

On the Cusp of Summer 34

The Bog House 36

Navigating the Water in Oak Bluffs 38

Fog Concert 40

Chappy 42

Waiting for the Rain 44

Farm Neck 46

Up-Island 48

Swan Feather Song 50

Close to the Elements 52

Vineyard Rain 54

Heat Wave 56

Clouds at Scrubby Neck 58

Love Is My Companion Now 60

Fireworks Night 62

Sea Wind 64

Fog Bound 66

Summer Ditty 68

On the Frontier of the Seasons 70

Last Days of Summer 72

Goodbye, Goobye to Summer 74

When Summer Ends 76

Vineyard September 78

IN THE DECADES OF THE SEASONS

I will argue that it is not necessary for a poem to mean anything outside itself. ...nothing in a good poem happens by accident...
—John Ciardi

Brooks Robards writes lyric poetry. We understand that to mean poems of discrete episodes, emotions, place, time; a genre to which the emphasis on narrative, in the late years of this century, has often turned its back, not to mention turned up its nose. Yet the lyric poem tells us about ourselves–our sensibilities–as much as the discursive poem.

The writer of this collection gives us alternatives and acceptances. She describes what she sees as beauty and, I am sure, would agree with another poet, the Pulitzer Prizer holder Mary Oliver, who says "...beauty is not madness—it is the challenge to be sane, to be thoughtful, to be wholesome." We are changed by the excitement and implication of it— beauty not just here on the Vineyard, where it is always at hand, but beyond, even in places and situations that we could deem its opposite.

Poetry, as we have it today, is about the self because the self is what we bring to experience–as writers and readers—our vision of, interpretation of, and response to our lives. Like musicians, we have line, pace and dynamics. Words are our notes and, like them are both design and discovery. Poems are also made up of technical stuff, the trifles of which Michelangelo said perfection is made. For those of us who practice poetry, this means diction, metaphors, rhythms, rhymes (internal and external, exact and tangential), and various devices that give our poems their structures.

Just as art always lives in the world it experiences, poets use techniques of the past in ways that reflect the freedoms and uncertainties of the present. Take a close look at Brooks Robards's poems; note how she frequently employs syllable count rather than metric feet to form her lines–it is a method found in the ancient traditions of Greek poetry as well as in the history and astounding variety of Welsch englyns. (Dylan Thomas, for all his denials, never absolutely forsook his native forms.)

Brooks Robards has undertaken to give us unsentimental visions of the island she loves and experiences in all its moods. Nothing has escaped her in the decades of the seasons she has spent here. Every person who lives as deeply as she with this or any island feels its weather–the fogs, rain, sun, wind–and its habitats. Our summer people, the committed ones, experience delight in being on-island underlain, even at arrival, by the sadness of departure. She evokes these feelings as well as the simply observed events of her days in Oak Bluffs and throughout the island: riding a horse, talking with a bereaved friend, watching fireworks; she reflects on a dead bird, old and new loves; and always the sea.

For those of us who feel as she does for this place, for those of us who haven't discovered it, and maybe even for people who don't respond to it, these poems always capture a special location, one self and our selves pleasurably and profoundly wherever we read them.

Poems are not irrelevant to life, rather, they define life. Build poems around images not messages; the messages will be there. In these ways, Brooks Robards's poems succeed remarkably.

—*Judith Neeld, Menemsha*

THE CEREMONY OF ARRIVING

I had forgotten how the trip
Transported me once, the rapture
Of slipping from one world into
Another replaced by routine.

This year, next to you, I relive
The urgency of entering
The ferry, watching from the deck
The languorous rush of water

As dock and land release their hold,
Becoming remoter, until
Passage itself swallows us up.
Then locking onto land again,

Car engines starting up and wheels
Clacking down the ramp to the dock
Where the crowd awaits reunion,
I can put aside memory

To join in the ceremony
Of arriving back on-island.

OPENING THE SUMMER HOUSE

May's chill abstracts clear skies;
No sound breaks a hush
In the air preceding
The change of seasons.
At least the house made it
Through winter intact.

Yellowed newspaper piles,
Dishes for two stacked
On the drain rack, clam rakes
Propped against a wall—
Relics from last summer
Etch on life's surface
Love's capricious retreat.

SUMMER'S FALSE START

Wind tops a surly ocean
With fresh dabs of whipped cream.
Battered greenery on trees
Struggles to find its way
Into the leavening sun.

For awhile harpy winds have
Won the fight for bleakness.
Sky's galaxy of grays mutes
The zest of the season;
Soon the island will sun dry.

O N - I S L A N D

Back on-island again,
I've unpacked and cleaned
My way to exhaustion;
Remnants of cold cling
Like leftover flies.
I get ready to sleep
In a draft-filled room
With lilac summertrees.

Outside, salt marshes stay
Drab; leaves are pallid.
Scotch Broom promises
Yellow blooms, but the wind
Sends spindrift onshore.
Foghorns will blow tonight.

A NEW SEASON

This island world is bare,
Washed in a new season,
Shadows dissipated

By the flood of bright light.
Even water's whitewashed
To patent-leather gloss.

Faint eruptions of green
Stay tamped by a sky packed
With pill-bottle cotton.

NOR'EASTER

Wind and rain on a rampage
Turn this island summer house
Into an eggshell fortress.
Walls fight each onslaught with creaks
And groans, talking to the wind.

Upstairs doors with a sea view
Cannot hold back the deluge
To the living room below.
Old windows funnel water
Into waiting floorboard seams.

Drips run along ceiling beams
To percussive pots and pans.
At last the roof itself lifts
Up so rain can worm its way
Inside at the right angle.

Giving in to the elements,
The house rides out the storm,
Wiser than its occupants,
Emerges swollen and damp,
To dry in the next day's sun.

EARLY MORNING
IN OAK BLUFFS

Day starts in silence,

Whitened, still steaming

In dew and a fog

That wants to linger.

Curtains lift and drop

With breezes en route

Through tree and trellis,

Away from the sea.

How will the day end?

Smoldering in haze,

Hovering on mists,

Or perched in the calm

Near scud's muted cloak

Of tide-bound places?

PLAISIR D'AMOUR
NE DURE QU'UN MOMENT

Old blue and the sun

Turn leaves green again.

Such simple beauty

Dresses up love's pain,

Like a rainbow's arc

At a shower's end

Or the moon at night.

Sadness will retreat

Yet keeps on haunting,

Until it speaks not

In the rain's silence

Or a tree's essence,

But finds an echo

In a French refrain.

LONGEST DAY
OF THE YEAR

Light bores down and cleanses
This longest day on the island.
Breezes snatch fresh laundry,
Line-dried, right out of waiting hands.
They stall, then spurt like weeds,
Keeping the season's heat at bay.

When the sun drops from sight,
Pulling darkness out of corners,
A solstice moon rises.
Ringed and limned with lunar masses,
It floods this shore-bound world
Once again with water-borne light.

WIND WATCH
IN OAK BLUFFS

Temporarily inside
And away from the water,
The poet moves headquarters
Into a back-of-the-house
Room, painted green and peeling.

Sounds in the kitchen below
From the rest of the family,
Breakfasting on blueberry
Muffins and tea, wander up
The back stairway with the wind.

Outside, breezes wash the air
Clean in a pale-palette sky,
Helping the sunlight turn crisp,
Prism-sharp corners around
Rooftops, fences and porch rails.

Only dark-needled branches
On the native pitch pines sway
With a rooted pliancy,
Intent on making music,
Steady in the wind's onslaught.

VINEYARD FOG

Fog creeps along the road

On the way from Scrubby Neck.

It numbs the heart, induces

Sleep, warms the night, as it curls

Through the scrub oak. Down-island

The cat kneads into my lap,

Claws back to his beginnings

With too-sharp talons. The fog

Makes a pillow to lean on,

If I can learn to lean.

STANLEY BURNSHAW PUTS HIS HOUSE ON THE MARKET

Fourteen rooms facing the cove;
Three-and-a-half baths. "Too big
Now with Leda gone. It's time

For a family—children,"
He explains. "It's too lonely
At night except for the cats

Chasing around and the stars."
He offers a painter's tour:
A drybrush by Picasso

Next to a watercolor
By a blind painter who marked
Her place with pieces of clay.

From the back porch, cove water
Rises, flat as cardboard flocked
With yarn whitecaps and sailboats.

Clouds pass, pendulant, above.
On the way out, Stanley points
To the sweet peas and rose bush

That his Leda used to tend,
Peppered with dried blooms. He says,
"Good. You parked in the right place."

S O L I T U D E

I made a shrine once
On a sand dune:
Three water-washed
Stones and a shell
To solitude.

The ocean
Drummed below.
Senseless, I thought,
When sand shifted
Over the fluted shell,

And the stones fell.
But I smoothed
The sand, lined up
The stones again
And propped the shell.

Was it habit,
I wonder,
Knowing only
That I must have
My shrine and solitude.

ON THE CUSP
OF SUMMER

Too low for clouds, too high for fog,
Vapors roil in the air overhead,
Invading the space above scrub oak
And pitch pine under open sky.

On the road to Deep Bottom Cove,
A deer's cloven hooves leave a clean line
Of prints along the tongue of soft sand
Running between ruts. Two more deer

Look up from grazing in a field
Of daisies, then leap into the brush.
An osprey, calling from aloft, dips
And rises, still tied to its nest.

Meandering turkey chicks grow
To such mass they rival their parents.
Swans on West Tisbury Pond shepherd
A single cygnet; crickets trill.

As summer hovers on the cusp,
Time passes without pause. Stillness marks
The season's shift, making the circuit,
Never the same, ever the same.

T H E   B O G   H O U S E

I finished up almost too late
To make my way to the bog house
For one final swim, then rode past
Its driveway, lost in memories.

Landmarks we had learned together
Slipped by unnoticed: white farmhouse
On the left, graveyard on the right,
Nest of mailboxes. Some endings

You can never be ready for.
Folded and stacked against the fence
At the driveway's end, stood the same
Wrecked lawn chairs, waiting for the dump.

The rope swing, electric yellow
And crooked, still hung in the dip
Across from the house. I walked past
To the beach path without stopping.

The gnats had fled, and the stream spilled
Calmly over cranberry dam,
Through culvert, into the pool where
We had bathed after making love.

From the headlands on the far side
Of the woods, I saw the ocean
Had grown rough, even in the cove;
Beachgoers were heading back home.

This time the changeable water
Did not scare me, the way it had
On the first day you took me out,
Not even seaweed slithering

Between my arms or the whitecaps.
I swam out two times: the first was
For you, to show myself I could
Still do it when you weren't there;

The second time was for pleasure.
Then I wandered barefoot across
Waterwashed stones strewn like marbles
Over the sand, up to the bluff.

Climbing up that rugged hill,
Out of breath, kicking on the shoes
I had left where the path travels
Through beach plum and poison ivy,

I turned back to look at the cove.
You—your absence—was everywhere.
Making my way back to the car,
I stopped to give the swing a try.

Then I forced myself to walk up
And peer through the windows the way
We had before discovering
You would move in and stay awhile.

The child's wooden wagon loaded
With plastic jugs for your water;
The oak table in the kitchen
Where you kept sea salt and heart pills;

The old blue throw on the day bed:
Such things stayed familiar
Like the summer season, not yet
Turned into strangeness and the past.

NAVIGATING THE WATER
IN OAK BLUFFS

Others abandon caution, dive
Head first into murky, viscous,
Fish-nudging, crab-nibbling depths.
Never me. I start with wading,
Seek out the softest waves, scuttle

Toes first past the last pebble-strewn
Ridge of land, searching for the sand
Beneath, free of seaweed and rocks.
The bottom drops off so gently,
I think I could keep on walking

To the place where the sky's blue sheet
Unites with white-crested water,
The sea still lapping my ankles.
Boat washes swell the waves to knees,
Then ebb. Not yet. Next thighs and back.

Wait! Crotch, at last. After the shock,
I consider bellying in
But stop. Another crest catches
The midriff offguard. Then again:
Even wetter a second time,

I step to rib depth. Now? Shoulders
Resist persistent salty slaps.
Arm swings practice lateral moves.
Knees bend. Aaiiee! Head up, I part
Water again with praying hands.

Cool fluid flows over each pore
Of bare skin. Waves wet hair and head.
I tread water, roll over, float,
Arms stretched wide, near Oak Bluffs harbor,
Watching the clouds churn overhead.

F O G C O N C E R T

Sunlight has struggled all day long

To weave its way through clouds and fog.

Stillness hangs in every corner

Of the island. On the wooded path

To the new school, skunk smells linger,

And mud with no inclination

To dry lies under the log walkway.

On guard around the Tabernacle,

Lace canopies of oak and maple

Shield picnickers from mists above

And the chill of onshore breezes,

So music can wander through the leaves.

C H A P P Y

A great blue skims Poucha Pond,
Setting down on marshy ground
Beyond the barrier beach.
Stretching up his snake-like head,
The heron scans the water,
Then takes wing again to land,

Safe in sedge across the way.
Patchworks of soil and water
Tuck his temporary cote
Into silent harmonies;
Chappaquiddick's long finger
Curls around, pointing westward.

WAITING FOR THE RAIN

After endless weeks

Of endless sunshine,

Clouds cover the sky.

Stiff winds chase a chill

Through the house and set

Pink geraniums

Swinging on the porch.

The cat curls up inside.

Rain withholds relief

Until day is done,

Waits to find its hour,

Planting random seeds

Of uncertainty,

Syncopating the night.

FARM NECK
In Memoriam: SMR

I took you golfing
On the course I loved,
With mown corridors
Lush as green carpet.

A large bird of prey
Stood by the first hole.
From the sea's closeness
I guessed an osprey.

Stationed above us
Next to a sandtrap,
He eyed us coolly
As he nudged his kill—

Mallard or seagull—
It was hard to tell.
Wind scattered feathers
Across the fairway.

We ended our play
While this predator
Waited to finish
His meal by himself.

The breeze died; water
Gleamed in the distance;
The air smelled of salt;
Trees were August ripe.

UP-ISLAND

Chatting busily in first light,
Geese sound an urgent wake-up call,
As a westward course pushes them
Past Chilmark Pond. Steady breezes
Haul cloud cover across clear skies,
Forecasting rain. Surf drums itself
Into a thunderous backdrop.

Among tangles of brush, brambles
And wildflowers—Butterfly Weed,
Black-Eyed Susan, Tansy, Thistle
And Queen Anne's Lace—nests a beach house.
Its windows frame still-blue snapshots
Of three swans winging down-island,
Droning throaty, airborne bouquets.

SWAN FEATHER SONG

Waterside, cars pass
By on the beach road
Blinded to a heap
Of stark white debris
Beside a salt marsh.

Anchored in the mud,
The dead swan's body
Rises like a sail,
With its wings still cocked,
Aiming for the sky.

Feathers alone thwart
The passage of flesh
Into sediment,
As if their whiteness
Could launch them again.

One by one, they lay
Their way on water,
Nest themselves in sedge,
Or, airborne, travel
Seaward with the wind.

CLOSE TO
THE ELEMENTS

Who peeled that sardine
Lid off Farm Pond sky,
Corralling the clouds
At horizon's line?

Sand blazes whiter
In squirming sunlight;
Speckled sea uncorks
Itself bottle green.

Such insular tricks
Catch sailors adrift
On Nantucket Sound
And looking to land.

VINEYARD RAIN

Rain plunges in glassine sheets
From porch rooftops into earth
Sucked dry by summer sunshine.
Hanging geraniums reel
From their sudden bath. Wind sweeps
Raindrops across tabletops,
Soaking chair cushions and seats,
Sending tourists into town.

HEAT WAVE

Sun beams itself laser-sharp,

Wearing out its welcome,

Draining every droplet

Of moisture from the soil.

Pastures catch fire, and horses

Escape into the pond.

Parched grass crackles underfoot;

Skin approaches meltdown,

Dries, then burns into the night.

Instead of rain's relief

A haze of heavy air spreads,

And fog sidles, crab-like,

Across an inlet, playing

Hide-and-seek with the light.

CLOUDS AT
SCRUBBY NECK

Clouds sail in water across the lagoon,

Next to marsh grasses naturally groomed.

Clouds pile up in a beauty-parlor sky,

Then float seaward without releasing rain.

Clouds fly as swallows loop the open plain,

And earth-bound guinea hens bob in circles.

Under clouds, wild turkeys weave their way home,

Leaving a trail of feathers as they roam

Across meadows where nests have been concealed

Of rabbits and other cloud-blind beings

Too intent upon routine for seeing

Clouds suspended above on summer skies.

L O V E   I S   M Y
C O M P A N I O N   N O W

after years alone
pressing chin
stomach palms thighs
into   icy sheets
i sink   into your flesh
make your sleep   mine

hear a catalogue
of   pleasures
first i soak up
warmth more bone-soothing
than hot tubs that follow
days spent on skis

then breast pressed to chest
knee on thigh
hip   to belly
my arches cup   your
toes each   with   each   your beard
tickles   my nose

lips chomp between   snores
legs shudder
hands lead   wheezes
into songs fashioned
out of sudden twitches
and random shakes

one night from a dream
you bellow
come in waking
us   out of the dead
stall of sleep to listen
as wind flaps   shades

spoon nested we while
away nights
in may pitched back
under cover with
blankets of love one   pressed
and pressing   flesh

FIREWORKS NIGHT

Since now the season's set to end,
Fireworks fly in celebration.
Sparks aim for the stars through chilly air,
Close to collision with passing planes,
Before they release their cascades.

Boat lights bob on Nantucket Sound,
Joining the dance against darkness;
The latest evanescent light moves
The audience to sighs and applause;
Windows rattle with explosions.

When the sky subsides into black,
A band plays on Ocean Park's edge,
Catching stragglers with serenades
To summer's almost bygone rhythms,
Mingling melodies with smoke.

S E A   W I N D

It was one of those days

When the wind blows,

And the sun comes and goes.

Field flowers splashed

Reflections in color

Of the heat; red

Roses turned magenta.

It would be a fine day

When the wind died,

But the blowing remained

To contend with,

And a heavy gray haze

Shrouding the sea

Made its way over me.

F O G   B O U N D

At the hour when fog stalks shrouded streets,

Turning corners into question marks,

I dream of greener days making seas

So brazen blue they mock unfurled skies,

Of salt marshes growing succulent;

Sand baked golden, butter-ready brown,

Until fog vanishes on a breeze,

Then, airborne again, brings down the sun.

SUMMER DITTY

In June the ear's attuned;
Sound makes the highest sense.
But, then, could it be
Touch that gives so much
To the nothingness
Of gentle breezes
On the barest of skin?

When the eye grows shy
From so much glory,
And tongues are sated
With its vernal sweet,
Could we make a case
For the nose who knows
New fragrance every hour?

I've learnt if it weren't
For cloudy respites
Or sudden showers,
Mind might devour
Sweet summer's beauty,
Pilfering with it
All of summer's power.

ON THE FRONTIER
OF SEASONS

This island, surrounded

By sunlight and water,

Is a place of comings

And goings, never still.

Perched on the frontier

Of seasons, it shocks us

With shifts from sun blazes

Into satin gray clouds.

LAST DAYS
OF SUMMER

After hurricane winds
Have blown themselves away,
Leaving behind a trail
Of broken chimes and blooms,
Summer's gentle breeze comes,
Reminder for awhile
Of time's uneven pace,
Grown leaden once again.

Under clarified skies
Nighttime's crickets call out
From the blackening leaves.
Ocean currents have ebbed,
And the sounds of ripeness
Sing farewell songs to fall.

GOODBYE, GOODBYE TO SUMMER

Pulling the eye down level
With the surfaces of things,
Sky simplifies its color,
Until you can disappear
Into late-August blue.

A speckled mirror, the sea
Rolls en masse below, repose
Released in activity.
Cricket chatter that starts up
At this time of year matches
The momentum of the wind.

Defying a universe
Where we imagine roundness,
The sun hangs too low to soak
Even this ripe, Island world
With summer heat and purpose.

Nor do mists of deception
Blur water's end. Sky defines
Its limits, and flocks of birds

Shower the beach like petals.
Having climbed or crawled as far
As the season will take it,

Vegetation darkens, tamed
Into completion for now;
A solitary dry leaf
Chases itself down the street,
Punctuating summer's end.

WHEN SUMMER ENDS

Like a lover grown bored,
Summer loosens its hold
On the Island. Wind takes
What's left of airborne warmth
And stirs the ocean
Into a whitecap broth.

A lone osprey inspects
The silent foliage
From his perch near dry fields,
Then takes wing and moves on.

Once day was all; now night
Calls. Shadows slice houses
And limp dogs, as if light
And dark can not unite.

The sun dies all day long,
Taking with it dazed flies,
And rabbits too engrossed
To dive into the brush.

VINEYARD SEPTEMBER

Honeysuckle sends its nectar
Into the cricket-laden air
Along the road to Edgartown.
Summertime's waning light fills up
The inkwell of sky plus water.

Tangles of undergrowth, luscious,
Exhausted in the season's pause,
Frame meandering salt grass flats
Across the road into Farm Pond.

Dark, silent, paying their tribute,
Gulls mass on Hart Haven pilings;
Cars hum along the sandbar strip;
Runners slap the black macadam;

Walkers march; planes buzz. No one stops
To mark the sun's shift slowly south.

Until next season...